NEW STONE

NEW STONE

MATTHEW FORBES

Copyright © 2014 by Matthew Forbes.

ISBN: Softcover   978-1-4931-5788-4
             eBook   978-1-4931-5789-1

All rights reserved. No part of this book may be reproduced or transmitted in any form or by any means, electronic or mechanical, including photocopying, recording, or by any information storage and retrieval system, without permission in writing from the copyright owner.

This book was printed in the United States of America.

Rev. date: 12/28/2013

To order additional copies of this book, contact:
Xlibris LLC
1-888-795-4274
www.Xlibris.com
Orders@Xlibris.com
144786

TABLE OF CONTENTS

A. A Soul to Speak 7
    Soul To Speak 9
    Kindred 10
    Cup of Welcome 11
    Pillars 12
    The World Inside 13
    Birth Right 14
    The Future 15
    The Past 16
B. The Naked I (I) 17
C. The Garden 18
D. Coincidence 19
E. The Naked I (II) 20
F. Be-Thyself 42
G. Devoted To Life 43
H. The Naked I (III) 45
I. Ancestors of the Future 46
J. The Blue Cloud 47
K. Notes to the Adventurer 49

A Soul to Speak

The myths are maps to guide the wandering stars

Matt

Soul To Speak

In the caves of old
Is written
The New Stone
Every Age seeks a Champion
A soul to speak
In a vivid dream the elder came to me
Spoke lovingly and said:
The Limited Trial of Memory
Leads You to the Limitless
Trail of Eternity

Kindred

I only speak when Im spoken through
I'v seen you freak and broken too
We ran beside the wild dogs back in our Youth
You came to play but trust in few
Earth kid out of think granted genius of mystic drink
Right brain life is the electric divide
Crimes loud virgin media hunts light
Just forget just feel I must heal minds
The silent kind defines all that is left
This nightly gift we steal a last love
Even when eyes shine dim and we slip
From skin the shell of the sin we pretend
And the truth we bend
In dreams my kindred crowd sings
Free time before mankind re-thinks
The last grains of hourglass humor
I lost mine to fast nights and the mirror
Myths & Gatherings to share our learning
Ancient Ideas to Guide our journey

Cup of Welcome

To the world of Mystics mortals and the dead
I offer the cup of welcome and wisdom
To be a favorite of the Gods
To have a guardian of the road
Wise counsel silence offers the soul
To rouse or calm the inner waves
To make the dead speak
And to gain mother natures love
A catalyst is the way to abandon
The escapist will change our world
Bestowed the vocation to influence
Mistaken originality, a persona, a teacher
Their havoc on habit, invoked by memory, comfort, outward clarity
Extinguish exhausted perceptions and invoke intuition
It's your subconscious speaking it's the chill down your back
Valued more then any worldly attribute
It speaks loud but numbs the senses
It's taking the blinders off

Pillars

Let one look guide the stars of the hearts that will
not fade and never part the truth before a lie is told
twice as sweet when will we meet the destiny at arms
length a blink of time and spill of the glass upon
the open door reflects the thoughts of the pillars
separating the tapestry of remembrance embrace
this spot of mine no trace left behind upon the field
to stand is to choose to sit is to abide a moment in
time the great follow the mystery step past the gate
stand alone to build a home a mask to hide your fate
will you ignore what's outside your front door is life
not satisfying of it is not death defying we believe
god looks down and doesn't complain I look up and
wonder if god ever had a name not quite someone
but all the same counting on you the few to blame
We wake to nothing and begin everything
Create the day and the way we play
Until the sun sleeps and it is time to retire by the
quiet fire
A narrator aspires to confess the calm of night is
blessed
Death tests if life is glass and interest reveals how
long until it cracks
To see the end yet everyday we wake to do it over
again

The World Inside

This rewinds a lifetime the many threads we tread
and in time we decide ones to web and others to wed
the art is of man only a narrow few remain to teach
the lessons to perceive is at once how can it be with
the eyes that by a whisker see
From the cradle to the fable stuck in the middle
between our self in the divine the entrance is a trail
traveling the mind belief carries us on the fabric of
imagination unborn the fade of time hold tight the
truth you seek the world is farther then we see larger
then we think the passion inside must be delivered
far and wide

Birth Right

To the world of Gods Mortals and the dead
It is said the soul came to make mortals of them
Giving breath a sight and the colors of life
One day the sound will announce the final battle
From the wreckage of the ancient
A new world was born

The Future

In regards to the future there is a mirror in your hands
an echo in the ear a beating of the heart
with the sun and moon for eyes
you are not to blame for the trouble and the pain
our world as a time tunnel
the mechanics of experience and desire push us to
inspire your message a secret passage of the heart
enter the garden of yourself cross the bridge of mystery
discover from big to small uncover yourself and all
breathe out and relax lift the soil of thought
to plant the future seed with mind and believe
you can do anything
take part in the organic dance of uncertainty
the romance of chaos and chance
we are all connected change outside is evolution within
take a closer look from far away
a time where there are no words to say
that star in the sky might be a reflection of your mind
in time and space a place of no culture or race to be
one only the love and fun between everyone

The Past

In regards to the past it never did last
we found out about the gift of now
a present
the moment of self that knows no other
when the earth is in trouble we can circle
obliterated
washed
and reincarnated
without competition
united in recognition
intuition will prevail over superstition
to break convention is the intention
travel to another dimension
we call it ascension
never fear the objection of introspection
the truth of soul reflection
The corruption began by putting a silence to silence
Create with determination
Set you hearts destination

The Naked I (I)

"Do not worry my star touched child; the path you are meant for is right before you. Do not let the judges stand in your way, do not listen to what they say, follow the clouds and all will be well."

The Garden

We must:
Be true to our word
Let moments unfold
To breathe
See everything from every side
To lead and let others lead
To let the song in our heart write itself
And to be the scribe of your life and time

With Glass Wings
The past is but a piece of broken glass
A shard from time that will not last

Coincidence

Is it a coincidence that a child can be raised without two parents and learn to trust and create a solid family
Is it a coincidence that a child told they would forever have a challenge to speak read and write can one day become a public speaker
Is it coincidence that a child can see loving elders pass on and from that learn eternal youth
Is it coincidence that a child after their first hurt in love can let go and forgive and know how to love another
with all their heart?
Is it coincidence that a child can loose their glasses and yet can still see the truth before them?
Is it a coincidence that there are no coincidences?
Now we can see our purpose

The Naked I (II)

"You are made up of so many energies. Do not confuse yourself by seeking ones that are not true, but feel blessed by the ones you possess. By comparing yourself to others, whom are you putting higher? By being the one true you, imperfect star kissed one, you are creating. No one can take that from you. Be as you are and all will fall into place. Your visions will come to sight; do not fear you are on the path to light . . ."

: ANCESTORS OF THE FUTURE :

BREAK THE CAGE, TAKE THE STAGE =

< THE LOUDEST SILENCE, YOUR SOUL TO SPEAK ^

> THE NAKED I, YOUR UNIVERSAL FACE *

THE LIMITED TRIAL OF MEMORY
LEADS
TO THE LIMITIESS TRAIL OF ETERNITY

YOUR LIFE WILL BE OF GOOD USE
IF YOU CAN TURN AGE INTO YOUTH
BEGINNING WITH IMAGINATION AND
CREATION

INSPIRE THE INDIVIDUAL
EVOLVE THE WORLD

OUR LIVES ARE GLIMPSES OF GREAT
MYSTERIES

THE TRUTH AMUSES WITH A LAUGH AND
CAN SHOCK WITH A THOUGHT
AFTER ENOUGH DOSES OF PARADOX A
PERSON CAN AWAKEN FROM:
THE ILLUSIONS OF CERTAINTY TRIVIALITY
AND TEMPORALITY
WE ARE ONLY VISITING

THERE ARE PSYCHIC PROBLEMS AROUND US
WE NEED MIND DOCTORS TO TAKE A
CHANCE
WE NEED A MIND MEDICINE TO GIVE US A
CHANCE
CHANGE THE MIND AND YOU CHANGE
THE LIFE

A MAP OF MANKIND:
FIRST MANKIND TOUCHED THYSELF, TO FEEL
SELF DISCOVERY DIRECTED MANKIND TO
KNOW THYSELF, TO THINK
THE FINAL STEP OF SELF~VOLUTION*:
TO BE THYSELF

BECOME YOUR EVOLUTION

WE HAVE NO REASON FOR REASON BUT
THE REASON OF REASON ALONE
    THIS TRADITION HAS PEOPLE FROZEN IN
                              FEAR
IF WE INSPIRE THE WORLD, IT WILL
CHANGE THE INDIVIDUAL

HISTORY HAS ESTABLISHED ITS FICTION
    THE MORALS ARE FOR MORTALS
THE IMMORAL WILL ALWAYS BE IMMORTAL
TO SOME IT IS RUDE TO CHANGE YOUR
        MORALS WITH YOUR MOODS

LIGHTS CAMERAS DISTRACTION
    IN THIS LIFE WE EITHER GET TO GIVE OR
                        GIVE TO GET
TO BE YOUR SELF IS **SOCIAL SUICIDE**
TO BE SOMEONE ELSE IS SELF HOMICIDE

*VOLUTION:
A SPIRAL OR TWISTED FORMATION OR
OBJECT:
SELF+EVOLUTION=SELF~VOLUTION

ABOVE AND BELOW THE TWO ARROWS
STOP
YOU ARE WITNESSING THE LAST TICKING
OUR CLOCKS **FUTURE SHOCK**

LIFE HAS THE ONLY DANGER
TO BE SERIOUS WITHOUT FOLLOWING
THE CURIOUS
AND A LITTLE DANGER CAN BEGIN A LOT
OF FUN

ALL THOSE PROBLEMS IN THE FUTURE
HAVE A SOLUTION
WE EITHER QUITE TEMPORARILY OR FINISH
COMPLETELY
WHAT IS STRONGER YOU OR YOUR
PROBLEM?

AT TIMES THERE WILL BE SOMEONE TO
DISAGREE
EXPLAIN GENTLY THAT THERE ARE MORE
PROBLEMS
THEN PEOPLE WITH THEM
AND THIS IS SOMETHING WE CAN ALWAYS
AGREE UPON

A PROBLEM COMES FROM FEAR
WHAT YOU FEAR MOST YOU WILL BRING
CLOSE

WE COME TO THIS LIFE AND ARE REJOICED
BY MANY
IN THE BACK OF OUR MINDS
THROUGHOUT OUR LIFETIME
THE PROBLEM COMES NEAR
WE ARE AFRAID TO LEAVE ALONE

ONCE YOU DESIRED THE AWE-SOME TRUTH
NOW YOU KNOW TO ASK FOR THE
AWE-WHOLE TRUTH
.......KEEP UP WITH ME NOW ....
YOUR WIT DESCRIBES THE OUTER WORLD
WISDOM DECIDES YOUR INNER WORLD

KEEP IN MIND
WALKING IN A HOME IS WALKING IN THE
MIND
IF YOU HAVE NO MIND THERE IS NO HOME

WE ARE ALL OUT OF OUR MINDS FROM
TIME TO TIME
IT IS CALLED THE BODY

LET GO OF THE FUTURE AND FORGIVE THE
PAST
IN TIME YOU CAN ONLY LAUGH OR CRY

AND IN BETWEEN WHEN IT IS SILENT YOU
ARE STILL ALIVE
THAT IS OUR PRESENT
THE GIFT OF NOW
TRAVELING IN CONSTANT BIRTH

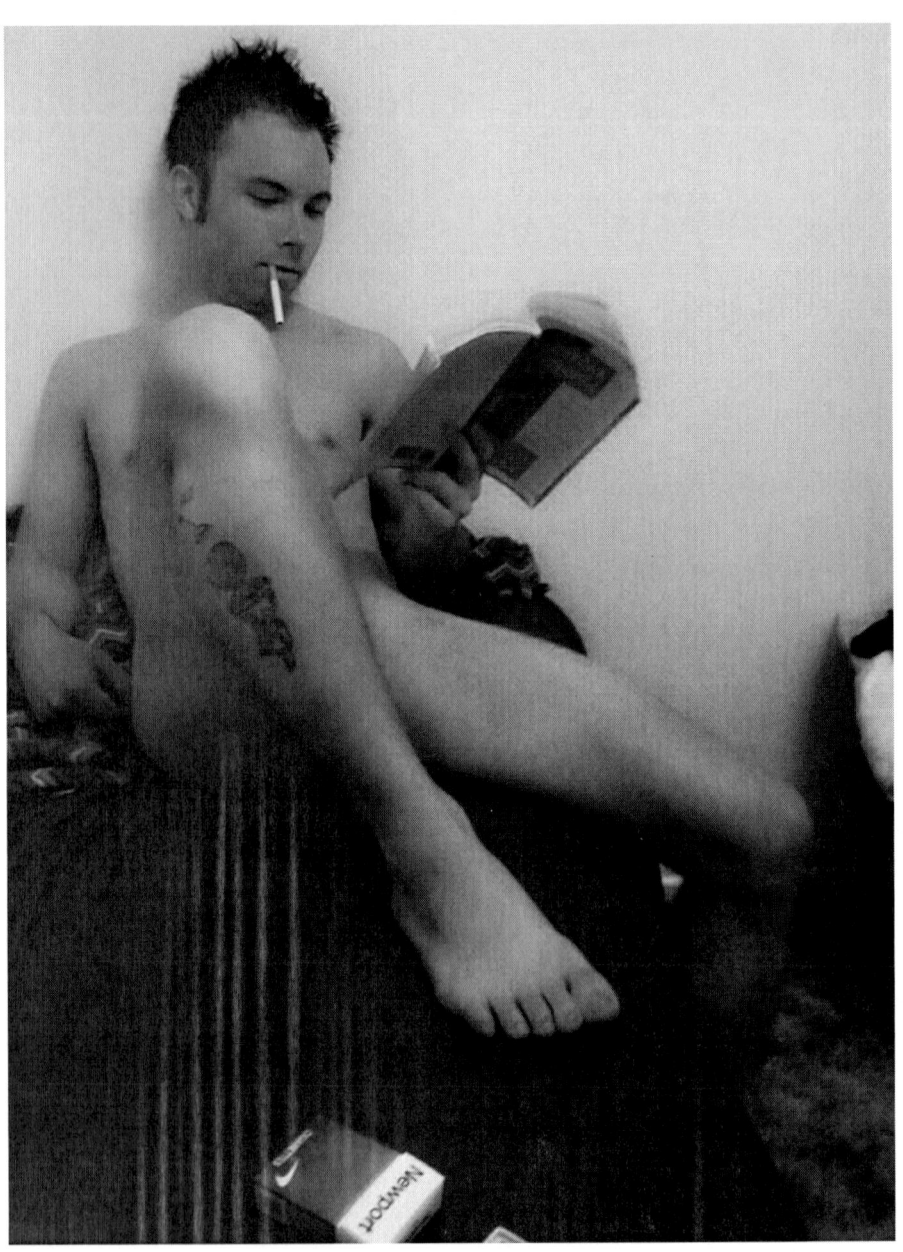

LIFE IS TOO SHORT
AND THE LIST OF PLEASURES TOO LONG

TO BE GOOD AT BEING BAD IS CHARM
TO BE BAD AT BEING GOOD IS TIRESOME

THE ROMANTIC REBEL IS CHARMING
BY ONLY VISITING AND NEVER CLINGING

THE TYRANT IS ANOTHER PEBBLE IN THE
DESERT OF FAILURE

THE CHARMING NEVER SPEAK THE TRIVIAL
THE DULL NEVER SPEAK ANYTHING BUT
THE TRIVIAL

THE CHARMING NEVER COMPLAIN OF THE
TRIVIAL
ONLY CONFUSED BY IT
THEY WORRY OF LIFE AND DEATH
THE DULL COMPLAIN AND WORRY OVER
THE TRIVIAL
AND ARE CONFUSED BY LIFE AND DEATH

I WOULD RATHER RISK LIFE AND DIE
GOING ALL THE WAY THEN LIVE NOT
RISKING ANYTHING

AND STILL DIE HAVING DONE NOTHING
AT ALL

YOU MUST LEARN THAT A LIE TO
SOMEONE ELSE
CAN BE A NEW TRUTH TO YOURSELF
ORIGINALITY KEEPS YOU YOUNG IT'S THE
TRUTH THAT CHANGES WITH THE OLD

SYMPATHY IS PITY AND EMPATHY
UNDERSTANDS THAT
REALITY IS A LIE-A LIE IS REAL-A LIE IS
ALIVE-TRUTH IS DEATH
MEMORY ILLUSION-A LIE IS CREATION-AND
FACT IS DECEPTION
LOGIC IS SIN AND A LIE IS LIBERATION

WHAT DO WE WANT?
CONFIRMATION-SENSATION-DESTINATION-
RELATION
FREEDOM AND LIBERATION
BUT WE ALL STAND AS A NAKED
INDIVIDUAL

AFTER ALL LIFE IS ONE F ADDED TO A LIE
THE F IS FOR FREEDOM BETWEEN I AND
THE LIES

FROM THE INTERNAL WE FEEL THE ETERNAL
AND
WONDER IF IT IS **MYTH OR LOGICAL**

BEFORE YOU ARE A FAMOUS FACE BECOME A FAMILIAR FACE

TO BECOME FAMOUS ALL YOU DO IS EXPRESS AND EMBRACE YOUR EXPERIENCE BIOGRAPHY IS DEATH-AUTOBIOGRAPHY IS ALIVE

THE UNFORGETTABLE WILL DIE FAMOUS
AND
THE FORGETTABLE WILL BE FAMOUS FOR DYING

WE ALL CELEBRATE LIFE IN FEAR IT MIGHT BE TOO SHORT
YET WE SELF-DESTROY OURSELVES FOR TOO LONG
BY TRYING TO FOOL OTHERS WE ONLY FOOL OURSELVES

WE ALL WANT CONTROL-TO BE ON TIME-PLAN IT OUT

WE CANNOT BE SUPERSTITIOUS OR
CURSED IF WE HAVE FREE WILL
ULTIMATELY YOU CAN ONLY CONTROL
YOURSELF
SO DON'T LOSE YOURSELF

WOMEN CREATED MAN TO PROTECT HER
IN THE WORLD
MAN CREATED SOCIETY TO CHANGE THE
WORLD
THEY CREATE CHILDREN TO CHANGE
SOCIETY AND PROTECT THE WORLD

THE NUMBER ONE IS BORN AND DIES A
NINE
WHILE ZERO GOES FULL CIRCLE WITH ALL
NINE COMBINED

LIFE IS CONCEALMENT
DEATH IS A SHADOW
AND BIRTH IS THE INDIVIDUAL

WHILE THE SQUARES ARE BUSY SQUARING
THEIR LIVES AWAY
IT IS THE RESPONSIBILITY OF THE CIRCLES
TO PROTECT THE SQUARES UNTIL THEY
COME FULL CIRCLE

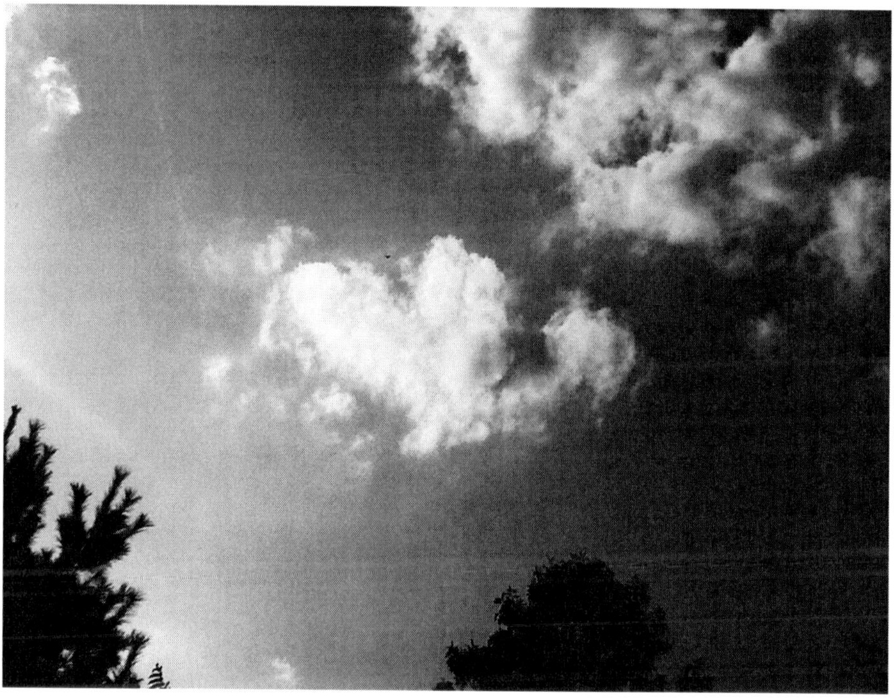

IN **THE STATE OF MIND**
THE INDIVIDUAL SEES ONLY THE OBVIOUS
OR THEY ARE OBLIVIOUS

MAKE AN EXAMPLE OF YOURSELF
DON'T BE MADE AN EXAMPLE OF

NEVER LET PEOPLE GET THE BEST OF YOU
IF THEY DON'T WANT THE BEST FOR YOU

NEVER WORRY ABOUT YOUR POSITION IN LIFE
OF FAMILY-WORK-SEX AND FRIENDS
AT DEATH WE ALL SHARE A PERMANENT POSITION

IN LIFE WE MAKE LOVE
AND FROM LOVE WE MAKE LIFE
        AND I AM NOT BEING FUNNY
I AM HAVING FUN AND THAT IS LOVE

LIVE TO SURPRISE

YOU WILL ALWAYS SURVIVE

NOT UNTIL WE KNOW NOTHING CAN WE
HAVE EVERYTHING
EVERYTHING WE HAVE BEGINS WITH
NOTHING

LEAVE HERE REMEMBERING WHO YOU ARE
WHERE YOU COME FROM AND WHERE
YOU ARE GOING

CLOSE THE EYE OF JUDGMENT-COME ALIVE
AND ENJOY YOUR TIME AS THE
INDIVIDUAL-LOVE LIFE
LOVE THE PEOPLE AND LOVE YOUR SELF

YOU CAN TURN AGE INTO YOUTH
WITH THE USE OF INSPIRATION AND
IMAGINATION-IT IS YOUR CREATION
INSPIRE THE INDIVIDUAL-EVOLVE THE
WORLD

BE-THYSELF

Devoted To Life

will I join the gods if I die is it worth life here does anyone want me near does I really matter anymore time is death fitted into thin sliced wedges of all great experience and lies and anything to fill the void truth is made up everyday that you wake up I want to speak to a god tell me something of meaning I'm done with my critics done with my dogma end with a question done with my needs or wants and they are all done with me this is the only answer the one to end it all it opens the gate to eternity I don't know if there's a devil or angel waiting for me from the same maker they came to be I was never prepared for this new way of living is it the only way I was going to do what they want what needs to be done why is it the one thing I love most at the same time shows all my flaws and insecurities I have never seen my end I have never felt oblivion I have nothing poetic to say the death would speak for itself but it does show that there is no freedom in another realm there are only more layers to the world I should have committed myself insane from the beginning I don't have a final

analysis on life or a solution I don't want one I exist
and it is there is nothing else to it where does it all
come from why cant I seem to better why is it so
unknowable and afraid and have to learn everything
why are there walls why learn what cannot be used
but only abused why is there why
Is there anything else to say this is a terrible excuse
for a suicide note no I know id write at least one in
this lifetime I never want to commit to death when I
will always be devoted to life and this mind of mine

The Naked I (III)

"Death is a friend. We cannot hide from change. You know, you have walked beside time. Allow the unknown in, but not too close. Retain control and distance until the time is right, and then greet the Eternal with open arms. Death is not always signifying life ends. It will bring change to you."

Ancestors of the Future

To the world of Gods Mystics Mortals and the dead
Patience taught them the magic formulas
None are equal in wisdom to the imagination
Acquired by questioning and exploring the wide
The mortal world is not eternal

One day the sound will announce
the final battle of time & death between life &
eternity

from the wreckage of the ancient
a new world was born
to them it was reserved to renew this world
their secrets shone
to wise creatures
the future was known

The Blue Cloud

Messenger of the sky circle my dreams invite me
into the cave where silence surrounds the answer
you gave there is fire in your eyes I will learn to
realize open me to heaven to heal me again tell me
the story so I know it well of how to attract and
how to repel help me to honor the gifts I give and
recognize my worthiness long as I live remind me
of innocence again with every man a brother and
each woman a friend teacher pathfinder of my soul
howling teaching me to know mystical as the moon I
will fly with you soon you know the secrets so very
well but you will never tell may I learn to hold my
tongue powerful yet silent with an enigmatic smile
you watch over the sands of forever teach me to
build my dreams hearts as one lessons learned break
illusion bring vision feel it filling all your needs
until your goal is reached know the inner power
that lies in your soul please stop your fright running
does not stop the pain or turn the dark to light so
freely you give of everything you are so others may
live power to run the open plains dancing in purple

dream rain will you dream with me travel across the stars beyond the place of time and space the visions from afar call the rains cleanse the earth fill me up again breathe with me breathe of divine universe in oneness we entwine experience renewal in the magic of living
Cycles of the whole a never-ending journey of the soul
Weaving webs of delight weave me a peaceful world
Souls take flight

Notes to the Adventurer

Remembered adventure takes on the quality of a dream
The more adventurous the adventure the more it fully realizes the idea the more dreamlike it becomes in our memory
Adventure begins when continuity with life is disregarded on principle
The adventurer is a historical individual who lives in the present
Adventure is a process of chance and necessity between fragmentary materials given us from outside and consistent meaning of life developed from within
The temporary asylum on earth with no real home means life is an adventure
Work is the inorganic relation to world, a grasp for opportunity regardless of harmony with the world or relation between the person and the world
Adventure is organic relation to the world; in conscious fashion it develops the world's forces and material toward culmination in human purpose
The adventurer: with strength and presence of mind gives complete self abandonment to accidents of the world which breaks duality of creation and destruction and shows continuity, the adventure was in a continuity beyond man made time, beyond fragmented memory

Edwards Brothers Malloy
Thorofare, NJ USA
March 18, 2014